This Grateful Hearts Journal
Belongs to

_____Amber_____

Grateful Hearts

Girl's Gratitude Journal

fleurette press
www.fleurettepress.com

designed with love in California

Copyright © 2021 All Rights Reserved

All About Me

I am 7 years old.

I attend Athens Acadmy School.

City I live in: Athens

My personality type: Sweet

My favorite person is: Cindy

My favorite thing is: Scient

My favorite phrase is:

When I grow up I want to be: a Scientist

Me in a sentence right now: A Kind, nice, sweet, and smart

Positive Affirmations

Positive affirmations can be used to overcome negative thoughts, encourage positive changes in your life, and cultivate an optimistic mindset. Whenever you need to, just pick a phrase that you like (or create your own!) and repeat it several times throughout the day, either by saying it aloud or writing it down. Our thoughts have a lot of power!

- I am strong, brave and resilient
- I'm still growing and I love who I'm becoming
- I am unique and beautiful in my own way
- I believe in myself and my abilities
- I am capable of amazing things
- I am strong enough to overcome any difficulty
- I am special and wonderful in my own way
- I forgive myself for my mistakes; my mistakes don't define me
- I deserve to be treated with respect and kindness
- I'm doing the best I can and that is good enough

Why Keep a Gratitude Journal?

Why should we take a few minutes each week to appreciate and write down the good things in our lives? Well, numerous studies have shown that doing this simple activity has so many amazing benefits! Practicing gratitude helps us:

- Feel happier
- Feel less stress
- Build healthy relationships
- Empathize with others better
- Build resilience to cope with disappointments better
- Stay positive even during difficult times
- Sleep better
- Have fewer health problems
- Improve overall well-being

Whew that's a lot of good that can come out of this! This journal will help you maintain a weekly habit of practicing gratitude and seeing the positive things in life. It's meant to be FUN, so let's get started!

TODAY IS:

How was your week? ☆ ☆ ☆ ☆ ☆

The BEST Things That Happened This Week

_____

_____

_____

_____

My Hopes for Next Week

I'm So Grateful For

. . . .

. . . .

. . . .

. . . .

No one else is you, and that is your superpower!

AWESOME!

We're all awesome in our own ways.
What do you think makes YOU awesome?
Don't be shy or humble here!

TODAY IS:

How was your week? ☆ ☆ ☆ ☆ ☆

The BEST Things That Happened This Week

_____

_____

_____

_____

My Hopes for Next Week

I'm So Grateful For

. . . .

. . . .

. . . .

. . . .

"Happiness and confidence are the prettiest things you can wear." - Taylor Swift

My Future FABULOUS Life

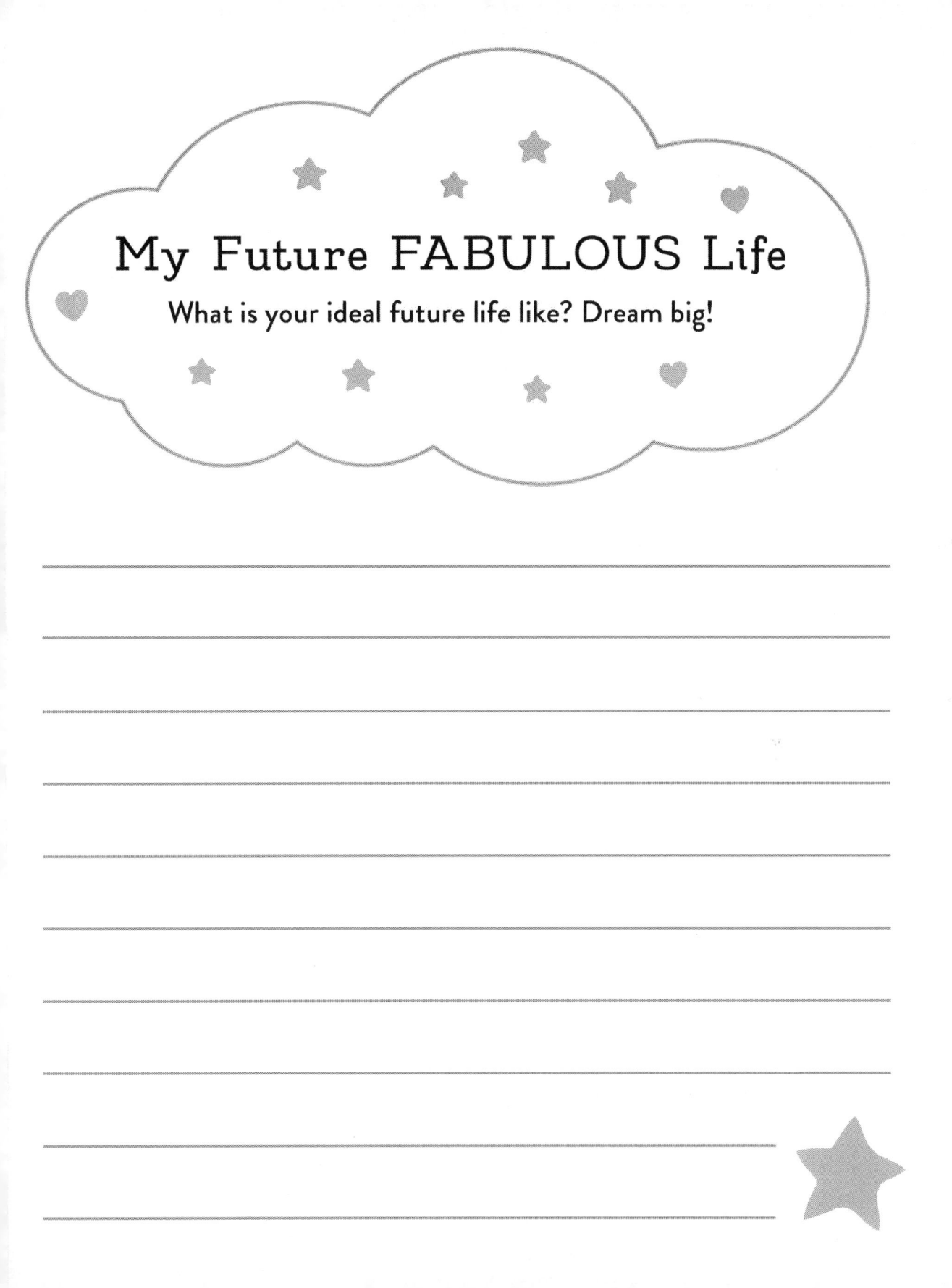

What is your ideal future life like? Dream big!

TODAY IS:

How was your week? ☆ ☆ ☆ ☆ ☆

The BEST Things That Happened This Week

_____

_____

_____

_____

My Hopes for Next Week

I'm So Grateful For

If at first you don't succeed, fix your ponytail and try again!

ADVENTURES

Life is an adventure - it can take you to so many places!
What are some of the places you'd like to visit?
What do you think it will be like there?

TODY IS:

How was your week? ☆ ☆ ☆ ☆ ☆

The BEST Things That Happened This Week

_____

_____

_____

_____

My Hopes for Next Week

I'm So Grateful For

Be your own kind of beautiful!

Who are you most grateful for in your life?
Describe what makes each person special.

TODAY IS:

How was your week? ☆ ☆ ☆ ☆ ☆

The BEST Things That Happened This Week

_____

_____

_____

_____

My Hopes for Next Week

I'm So Grateful For

Be HAPPY, be BRIGHT, be YOU!

List 5 Things That Make You Very Happy

Make sure to keep this list in mind
if you ever feel down about anything!

1. _____

2. _____

3. _____

4. _____

5. _____

LOVE

TODAY IS:

How was your week? ☆ ☆ ☆ ☆ ☆

The BEST Things That Happened This Week

My Hopes for Next Week

I'm So Grateful For

The day you start believing in yourself is the day magic starts to happen.

HOBBIES

Hobbies allow us to develop our interests and skills.
Some of your hobbies may even turn into a career!
What are some of your favorite hobbies?
Can you see any of them becoming a career for you?
Are there other hobbies you'd like to learn?

TODAY IS:

How was your week? ☆ ☆ ☆ ☆ ☆

The BEST Things That Happened This Week

_____

_____

_____

_____

My Hopes for Next Week

I'm So Grateful For

Strong girls don't put others down, they lift them up!

INSPIRATIONS

What are some things that really inspired you lately?
A song, a beautiful view, some cool architecture?
Always keep your eyes and heart open to new inspiration every day!

LOVE

TODAY IS:

How was your week? ☆ ☆ ☆ ☆ ☆

The BEST Things That Happened This Week

_____

_____

_____

_____

My Hopes for Next Week

I'm So Grateful For

. . . .

. . . .

. . . .

. . . .

Yes girl, you CAN!

What is the most beautiful place you have been to? Describe it and relive it now!

TODAY IS:

How was your week? ☆ ☆ ☆ ☆ ☆

The BEST Things That Happened This Week

_____

_____

_____

_____

My Hopes for Next Week

I'm So Grateful For

....

....

....

....

Shine with all your light and show the world your sparkle!

What are some of your BEST MEMORIES of the past month?

LOVE

LOVE

Day Full of Love

TODAY IS:

How was your week? ☆ ☆ ☆ ☆ ☆

The BEST Things That Happened This Week

_____

_____

_____

_____

My Hopes for Next Week

I'm So Grateful For

....

....

....

....

Why be a damsel in distress and wait for a Prince Charming when you can be a boss lady and be someone's Queen?

List 5 Things That You Like About Your Personality

Are there any parts that you want to make even better?

1. _____

2. _____

3. _____

4. _____

5. _____

TODAY IS:

How was your week? ☆ ☆ ☆ ☆ ☆

The BEST Things That Happened This Week

_____

_____

_____

_____

My Hopes for Next Week

I'm So Grateful For

....

....

....

....

Life will surprise you in the most wonderful ways!

NATURAL WONDERS

What are your favorite ways to enjoy nature?
Local parks, hiking, having fun at the beach, gardening?
Connecting with nature is good for us physically, mentally
and emotionally - make sure you get enough of it!

TODOY IS:

How was your week? ☆ ☆ ☆ ☆ ☆

The BEST Things That Happened This Week

_____

_____

_____

_____

My Hopes for Next Week

I'm So Grateful For

Let your dreams be as big as your desire to succeed.

Rate Yourself!

A healthy mindset is one of the keys to happiness.
How would you rate yourself in the following areas?
5 hearts if you completely agree!

♡ ♡ ♡ ♡ ♡

I believe in myself and my dreams.

♡ ♡ ♡ ♡ ♡

I am kind & grateful and I try to spread love & joy.

♡ ♡ ♡ ♡ ♡

I'm doing my best and I know that is enough.

♡ ♡ ♡ ♡ ♡

I'm still growing, but I love myself the way I am now.

♡ ♡ ♡ ♡ ♡

I know that my mistakes don't define me and
I forgive myself for them.

TODAY IS:

How was your week? ☆ ☆ ☆ ☆ ☆

The BEST Things That Happened This Week

_____

_____

_____

_____

My Hopes for Next Week

I'm So Grateful For

- - - - - - - - - - - - - - - - - - - -

- - - - - - - - - - - - - - - - - - - -

- - - - - - - - - - - - - - - - - - - -

- - - - - - - - - - - - - - - - - - - -

"If you are always trying to be normal, you'll never know how amazing you can be." – Maya Angelou

What skills are you proud of? Are you good at dancing? Drawing or lettering? Playing a musical instrument? Being a good friend?

TODAY IS:

How was your week? ☆ ☆ ☆ ☆ ☆

The BEST Things That Happened This Week

_____

_____

_____

_____

My Hopes for Next Week

I'm So Grateful For

_____

_____

_____

_____

Start each day with a smile and a grateful heart!

So Sweet!

Write about something you saw recently that warmed your heart.

TODAY IS:

How was your week? ☆ ☆ ☆ ☆ ☆

The BEST Things That Happened This Week

_____

_____

_____

_____

My Hopes for Next Week

I'm So Grateful For

....

....

....

....

"No one can make you feel inferior without your consent."
– Eleanor Roosevelt

List 5 Things That You Like About Your Home and Neighborhood

1. _____

_____

2. _____

_____

3. _____

_____

4. _____

_____

5. _____

_____

TODAY IS:

How was your week? ☆ ☆ ☆ ☆ ☆

The BEST Things That Happened This Week

_____

_____

_____

_____

My Hopes for Next Week

I'm So Grateful For

. . . .

. . . .

. . . .

. . . .

"All our dreams can come true, if we have the courage to pursue them." - Walt Disney

Thank You!

Write about a time someone went out of their way to help you. Has it inspired you to help others that need help?

TODAY IS:

How was your week? ☆ ☆ ☆ ☆ ☆

The BEST Things That Happened This Week

_____

_____

_____

_____

My Hopes for Next Week

I'm So Grateful For

. . . .

. . . .

. . . .

. . . .

"I never dreamed about success. I worked for it." – Estée Lauder

So Good!

What's one area in life that you're doing well in right now?

TODAY IS:

How was your week? ☆ ☆ ☆ ☆ ☆

The BEST Things That Happened This Week

_____

_____

_____

_____

My Hopes for Next Week

I'm So Grateful For

. . . .

. . . .

. . . .

. . . .

"I found that ultimately if you truly pour your heart into what you believe in, even if it makes you vulnerable, amazing things can and will happen." - Emma Watson

What are some of your BEST MEMORIES of the past month?

TODAY IS:

How was your week? ☆ ☆ ☆ ☆ ☆

The BEST Things That Happened This Week

_____

_____

_____

_____

My Hopes for Next Week

I'm So Grateful For

....

....

....

....

"Find something you're passionate about and keep tremendously interested in it" – Julia Child

Self Care

It's important to take care of yourself! What are 5 things that help you to relax when you're feeling stressed out? Some things may be listening to music, visiting a park, baking, or creating art. Find out what works for you!

1. _____

2. _____

3. _____

4. _____

5. _____

TODAY IS:

How was your week? ☆ ☆ ☆ ☆ ☆

The BEST Things That Happened This Week

_____

_____

_____

_____

My Hopes for Next Week

I'm So Grateful For

....

....

....

....

"If you push through that feeling of being scared, that feeling of taking risk, really amazing things can happen." - Marissa Mayer

My Favorites
Things I LOVE!

Song _____

Book _____

Movie _____

TV Show _____

Food _____

Dessert _____

Clothing Store _____

Restaurant _____

Animal/Pet _____

School Subject _____

Sport _____

Actress _____

Actor _____

TODAY IS:

How was your week? ☆ ☆ ☆ ☆ ☆

The BEST Things That Happened This Week

_____

_____

_____

_____

My Hopes for Next Week

I'm So Grateful For

. . . .

. . . .

. . . .

. . . .

"No matter how many mistakes you make or how slow you progress, you are still way ahead of everyone who isn't trying." - Tony Robbins

What are some of your life dreams?
What do you hope to accomplish or achieve?
Write them out!

TODAY IS:

How was your week? ☆ ☆ ☆ ☆ ☆

The BEST Things That Happened This Week

_____

_____

_____

_____

My Hopes for Next Week

I'm So Grateful For

"Success is no accident. It is hard work, perseverance, learning, studying, sacrifice and most of all, love of what you are doing or learning to do."
– Pele

My Favorite Color

What is your favorite color? Why do you feel a connection to it?

Do you agree with some of the common color associations?

- Yellow - happiness, optimism
- Red - boldness, passion, energy
- Blue - trust, loyalty
- Green - harmony, growth
- Orange - enthusiasm, youthfulness, emotion, optimism
- Turquoise - calmness, clarity, compassion
- Purple - spirituality, imagination
- Pink - love, compassion, femininity, playfulness
- Brown - stability, reliability, honesty, comfort
- Black - power, sophistication
- White - purity, innocence, perfection
- Gray - compromise, control, practical

TODAY IS:

How was your week? ☆ ☆ ☆ ☆ ☆

The BEST Things That Happened This Week

_____

_____

_____

_____

My Hopes for Next Week

I'm So Grateful For

. . . .

. . . .

. . . .

. . . .

"No matter what anybody tells you, words and ideas can change the world." - Robin Williams

What are your favorite things to do with your friends?

TODAY IS:

How was your week? ☆ ☆ ☆ ☆ ☆

The BEST Things That Happened This Week

_____

_____

_____

_____

My Hopes for Next Week

I'm So Grateful For

....

....

....

....

Some days you just have to create your own sunshine!

IMPORTANT!

What is one life skill you have learned that you'd like to teach others? Why is it important?

TODAY IS:

How was your week? ☆ ☆ ☆ ☆ ☆

The BEST Things That Happened This Week

_____

_____

_____

_____

My Hopes for Next Week

I'm So Grateful For

. . . .

. . . .

. . . .

. . . .

"There are only two ways to live your life. One is as though nothing is a miracle. The other is as though everything is a miracle."
- Albert Einstein

Seasons

There is beauty in all the season.
Spring flowers, warm Summer days,
Autumn leaves, cozy Winter nights and holidays
What are your favorite things about each season?
Do you have a favorite one?

TODAY IS:

How was your week? ☆ ☆ ☆ ☆ ☆

The BEST Things That Happened This Week

_____

_____

_____

_____

My Hopes for Next Week

I'm So Grateful For

"Those who don't believe in magic will never find it." - Roald Dahl

LOL

Describe a time when you laughed so hard that your belly hurt!

KEEP

GOING

Keep

Growing

You are Capable of *Amazing* Things

TODAY IS:

How was your week? ☆ ☆ ☆ ☆ ☆

The BEST Things That Happened This Week

_____

_____

_____

_____

My Hopes for Next Week

I'm So Grateful For

....

....

....

....

"Be kind whenever possible. It is always possible." – Dalai Lama

What are some of your BEST MEMORIES of the past month?

TODAY IS:

How was your week? ☆ ☆ ☆ ☆ ☆

The BEST Things That Happened This Week

_____
_____
_____
_____

My Hopes for Next Week

I'm So Grateful For

....
....
....
....

Be patient with yourself. Nothing in nature blooms all year.

Write a Thank You note to someone who was nice to you recently. Practice here!

TODAY IS:

How was your week? ☆ ☆ ☆ ☆ ☆

The BEST Things That Happened This Week

_____

_____

_____

_____

My Hopes for Next Week

I'm So Grateful For

"The expert in anything was once a beginner." – Helen Hayes

Who is your favorite teacher? Why?
What type of teacher would you be?

TODAY IS:

How was your week? ☆ ☆ ☆ ☆ ☆

The BEST Things That Happened This Week

_____
_____
_____
_____

My Hopes for Next Week

I'm So Grateful For

. . . .
. . . .
. . . .
. . . .

"The most certain way to succeed is always to try just one more time." – Thomas A. Edison

Who is someone famous that inspires you?
How does this person inspire you?

TODAY IS:

How was your week? ☆ ☆ ☆ ☆ ☆

The BEST Things That Happened This Week

_____

_____

_____

_____

My Hopes for Next Week

I'm So Grateful For

- -

- -

- -

- -

Don't give up, the beginning is always the hardest.

What is your happiest childhood memory?
Describe it and relive it now!

LOVE

TODAY IS:

How was your week? ☆ ☆ ☆ ☆ ☆

The BEST Things That Happened This Week

_____

_____

_____

_____

My Hopes for Next Week

I'm So Grateful For

....

....

....

....

If you see someone without a smile, give them one of yours!

What are your favorite things to do with your family? Why?

LOVE

TODAY IS:

How was your week? ☆ ☆ ☆ ☆ ☆

The BEST Things That Happened This Week

_____

_____

_____

_____

My Hopes for Next Week

I'm So Grateful For

....

....

....

....

"Creativity is contagious. Pass it on!" – Albert Einstein

Nature Walks

Being outside surrounded by nature is important for our physical, mental and emotional health. Describe your favorite park. What do you like to do there? Which local, State or National parks do you want to visit in the future?

TODAY IS:

How was your week? ☆ ☆ ☆ ☆ ☆

The BEST Things That Happened This Week

_____

_____

_____

_____

My Hopes for Next Week

I'm So Grateful For

....

....

....

....

When it rains, look for the rainbows.
When it's dark, look for the stars.

My Besties

Who are your 3 best friends or favorite classmates? Describe their personalities and what you like most about them.

1.

2.

3.

TODAY IS:

How was your week? ☆ ☆ ☆ ☆ ☆

The BEST Things That Happened This Week

_____

_____

_____

_____

My Hopes for Next Week

I'm So Grateful For

_____

_____

_____

_____

Shoot for the moon. Even if you miss, you'll land amongst the stars.

My Garden

Growing a garden is a great way to connect with nature
and also grow some food or flowers for yourself!
What would you grow in your garden?
Sketch a plan of it now!

TODAY IS:

How was your week? ☆ ☆ ☆ ☆ ☆

The BEST Things That Happened This Week

_____

_____

_____

_____

My Hopes for Next Week

I'm So Grateful For

"Never bend your head. Hold it high. Look the world straight in the eye." – Helen Keller

What are some of your BEST MEMORIES of the past month?

TODAY IS:

How was your week? ☆ ☆ ☆ ☆ ☆

The BEST Things That Happened This Week

_____
_____
_____
_____

My Hopes for Next Week

I'm So Grateful For

....
....
....
....

"Try to be a rainbow in someone's cloud." - Maya Angelou

Kindness Challenges

People who are treated with kindness are happier and are more likely to treat others with kindness. Brainstorm some things to add to this list of Kindness Challenges!

1. Make someone laugh today
2. Write someone a thank you note
3. Include someone new in your games or activities
4.
5.
6.
7.
8.
9.
10.

TODAY IS:

How was your week? ☆ ☆ ☆ ☆ ☆

The BEST Things That Happened This Week

_____

_____

_____

_____

My Hopes for Next Week

I'm So Grateful For

"The power you have is to be the best version of yourself you can be, so you can create a better world." - Ashley Rickards

You Go, Girl!

Doesn't it feel great when someone says something encouraging to you? It builds our confidence and makes us happy. What are some encouraging words that you're received recently? Is there someone that you feel could use some encouragement?

TODAY IS:

How was your week? ☆ ☆ ☆ ☆ ☆

The BEST Things That Happened This Week

My Hopes for Next Week

I'm So Grateful For

Don't stop until you're proud.

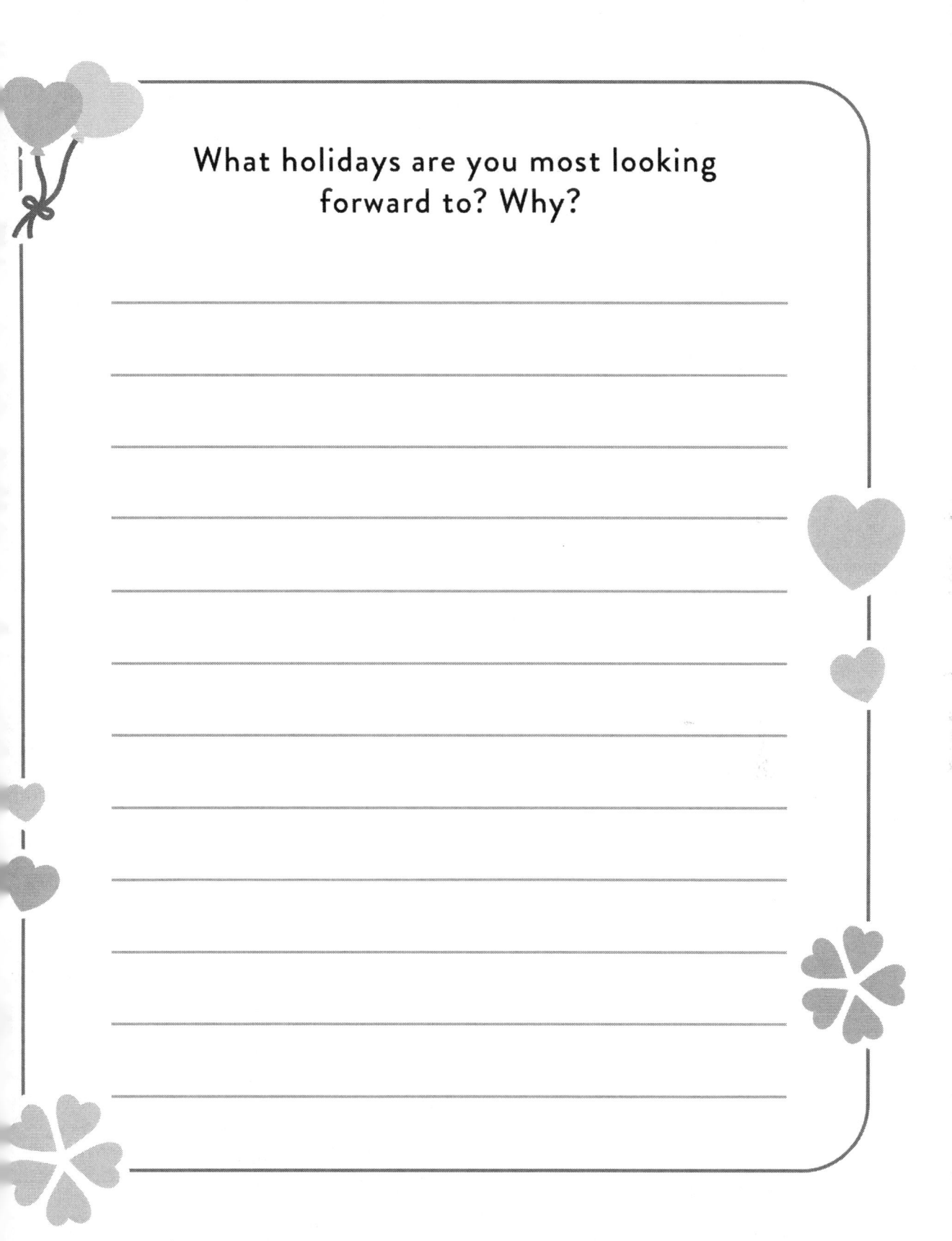

What holidays are you most looking forward to? Why?

TODAY IS:

How was your week? ☆ ☆ ☆ ☆ ☆

The BEST Things That Happened This Week

_____

_____

_____

_____

My Hopes for Next Week

I'm So Grateful For

You are amazing. Remember that.

Who is someone you know that you admire?
What qualities do you admire about this person?
How do you want to be like this person?

TODAY IS:

How was your week? ☆ ☆ ☆ ☆ ☆

The BEST Things That Happened This Week

My Hopes for Next Week

I'm So Grateful For

Keep shining beautiful one, the world needs your light.

Everybody likes to feel appreciated for their work and their contributions. Who is someone you feel is underappreciated? Is there anything you can do to show your appreciation?

Thank You!!

TODAY IS:

How was your week? ☆ ☆ ☆ ☆ ☆

The BEST Things That Happened This Week

My Hopes for Next Week

I'm So Grateful For

Every accomplishment starts with the decision to try.

My One Year Goals

Aim high and make things happen!
Write down 3 goals you'd like to achieve in the next year
and the steps you need to take to achieve those goals.

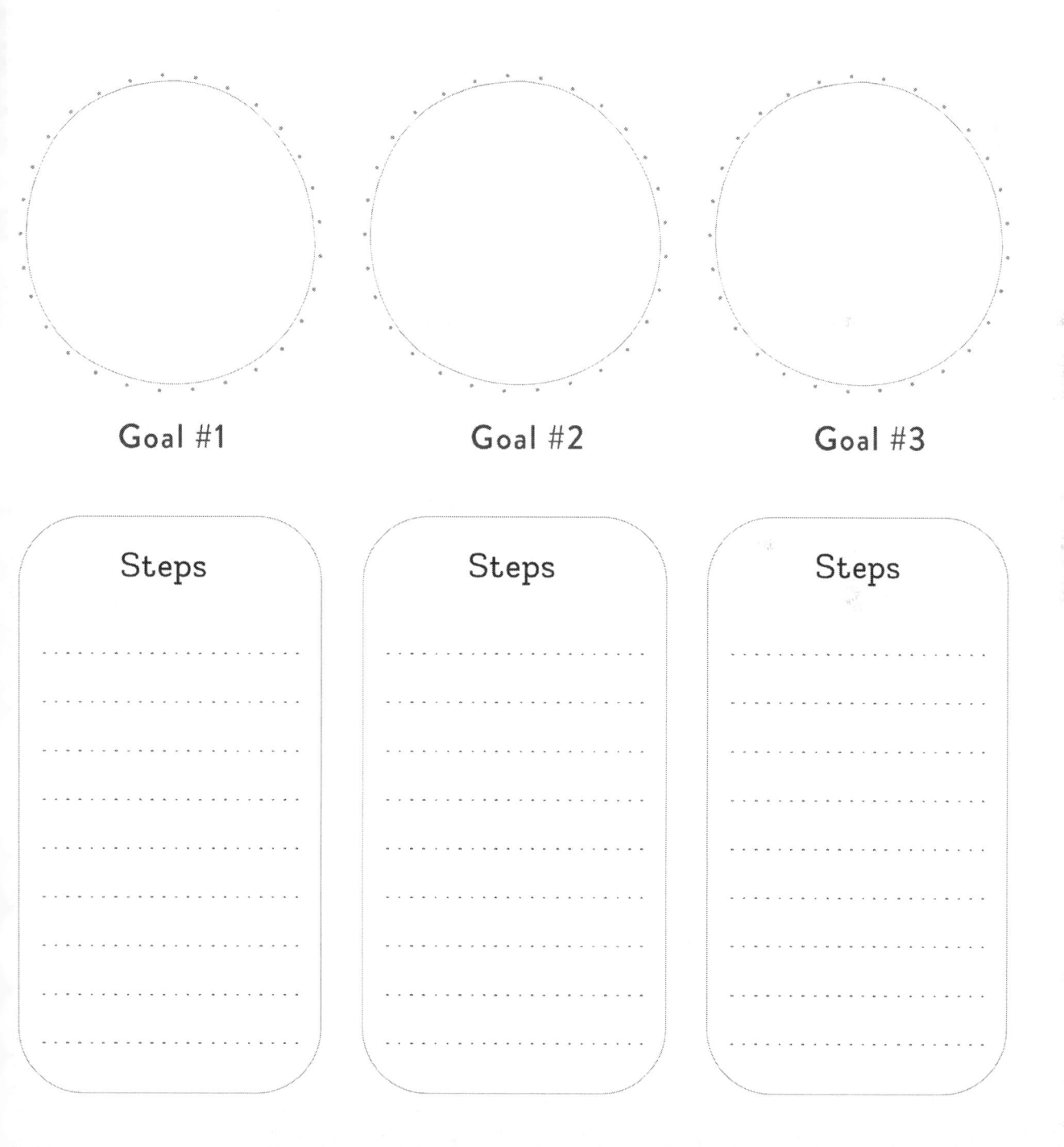

Goal #1

Goal #2

Goal #3

Steps

Steps

Steps

TODAY IS:

How was your week? ☆ ☆ ☆ ☆ ☆

The BEST Things That Happened This Week

_____

_____

_____

_____

My Hopes for Next Week

I'm So Grateful For

....

....

....

....

"Whatever you are, be a good one." - Abraham Lincoln

Project Surprise Kindness

Plan a special surprise for someone to brighten their day!
What will you do? Bake homemade cookies?
Make friendship bracelets?

TODAY IS:

How was your week? ☆ ☆ ☆ ☆ ☆

The BEST Things That Happened This Week

_____

_____

_____

_____

My Hopes for Next Week

I'm So Grateful For

_____

_____

_____

_____

Don't be afraid of being a beginner. We all have to start somewhere!

Write a short poem or song about something that amazes you. Isn't it fun to be creative?

TODAY IS:

How was your week? ☆ ☆ ☆ ☆ ☆

The BEST Things That Happened This Week

_____

_____

_____

_____

My Hopes for Next Week

I'm So Grateful For

Good things come to those who ~~wait~~ work for it.

What are some of your BEST MEMORIES of the past month?

TODAY IS:

How was your week? ☆ ☆ ☆ ☆ ☆

The BEST Things That Happened This Week

_____

_____

_____

_____

My Hopes for Next Week

I'm So Grateful For

Strive to be a person that you can be extremely proud of!

It's important to check in with yourself regularly, to acknowledge your feelings and needs. Complete the following sentences and add your own if you want.

I feel

I need

I wish

I celebrate

I worry about

I want to let go of

I forgive

TODAY IS:

How was your week? ☆ ☆ ☆ ☆ ☆

The BEST Things That Happened This Week

_____

_____

_____

_____

My Hopes for Next Week

I'm So Grateful For

....

....

....

....

You don't have to be perfect to be amazing!

My Dream Home

What does your dream home look like? Where is it located? In a big city? In a suburb? Near a beach? A house in the countryside? Sketch a home that you would like to live in. Include a floor plan!

TODAY IS:

How was your week? ☆ ☆ ☆ ☆ ☆

The BEST Things That Happened This Week

_____

_____

_____

_____

My Hopes for Next Week

I'm So Grateful For

She turned her can'ts into cans, and her dreams into plans!

What is something nice that someone did for you or said to you recently?

TODAY IS:

How was your week? ☆ ☆ ☆ ☆ ☆

The BEST Things That Happened This Week

_____

_____

_____

_____

My Hopes for Next Week

I'm So Grateful For

....

....

....

....

"Success is liking yourself, liking what you do, and liking how you do it." – Maya Angelou

What are some of your favorite books?
What do you like about them?

TODAY IS:

How was your week? ☆ ☆ ☆ ☆ ☆

The BEST Things That Happened This Week

_____

_____

_____

_____

My Hopes for Next Week

I'm So Grateful For

....

....

....

....

*"You don't have to be great to start.
But you have to start to be great." - Mark Twain*

What do you value in a friend? Do you try to be the same type of friend to others?

TODAY IS:

How was your week? ☆ ☆ ☆ ☆ ☆

The BEST Things That Happened This Week

_____
_____
_____
_____

My Hopes for Next Week

I'm So Grateful For

Be that kind soul that makes everybody feel like a somebody.

Make a List!

Things I Want To Do More Of

Things I Want To Do Less Of

TODAY IS:

How was your week? ☆ ☆ ☆ ☆ ☆

The BEST Things That Happened This Week

_____

_____

_____

_____

My Hopes for Next Week

I'm So Grateful For

Dream BIG, be BRAVE, show KINDNESS.

My 5 Year Goals

Aim high and make things happen!
Write down 3 goals you'd like to achieve in the next 5 years
and the steps you need to take to achieve those goals.

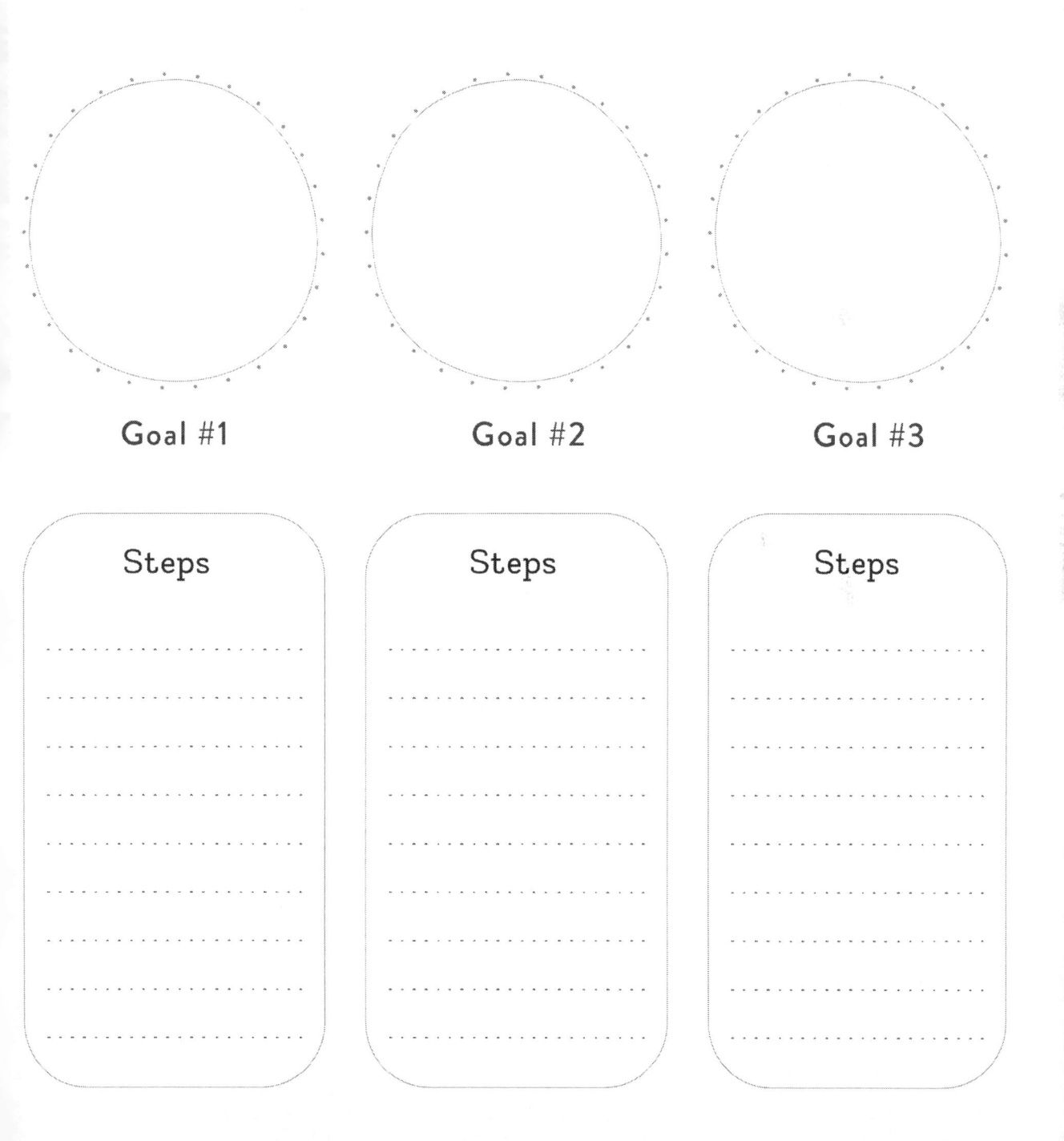

Goal #1

Goal #2

Goal #3

Steps

Steps

Steps

Made in the USA
Columbia, SC
06 March 2021